D0123900

This book is dedicated to some amazing women.

First, to my incredible Minnesota Mastermind group - Cathy Schmidt, Sarah Sladek, Kris Finger, and Julie Kimble: Your successes continue to inspire me.

Second, to my Speaker Mastermind group – Mimi Brown and Kim Becking: I'm so fortunate to have this amazing, mighty little group of fellow speakers who 'get' me!

Third, to my 3rd grade teacher, Ruth Quick, for seeing something in me all those years ago, and making this quiet girl feel special.

Lastly, to my wonderful friend and editor, Tracey Smith, who's been with me since our early Minnesota days.

Table of Contents

Introduction

I'm worried. I've looked out on the sales horizon, and the forecast isn't good. There's a huge change brewing, and it's set to fundamentally change sales and marketing as we know them.

If you've been in sales or marketing for more than 10 years, you know what I'm talking about—you feel the change. Buyers aren't responding the way they used to. They're becoming masters at ignoring you, and it's harder than ever for you to form relationships today.

---

*The tools that used to
work so well for you are
no longer producing
the same results.*

For marketers, reaching the customer through a media haze is becoming harder and harder. You're having to shift everything: your processes, your timing, your media outlets, the way you write your messaging, the photos you select...everything.

For those in sales, you may have a boss who calls it "a numbers game" and thinks you just need to work harder (I'm guessing that boss of yours hasn't been on the front line of sales in a long while, so they're giving you outdated advice, but more on that later).

Your marketplace may have more competitors than ever, fighting for the same business. Yes, there's definitely a change brewing.

It may seem severe or alarmist, but I believe that 80% of salespeople face losing their jobs in the next 10 years if they don't adapt. I'm generally referring to those in business-to-business (B2B) sales, but I believe all salespeople should take heed.

There's been a seismic shift in buyer behavior since the Great Recession, and it has set the stage for a massive restructuring of not only how salespeople sell, but when and why. I foresee a lot of fallout in the sales industry, unless salespeople can adapt.

Don't Become Extinct!

Why You Should Read This Book

Within the pages of this book are the solutions to help you not only survive, but adapt and get ahead. You may think, "This doesn't apply to me," but every sales and marketing person can find takeaways here. This information is coming from your target customers, and they're speaking to me loud and clear. I'm not only the messenger, though; I have a 20-plus-year history as a million-dollar buyer. Believe me when I say that change is happening now.

If you're fortunate to be in a seller's market in your industry, congratulations! In a seller's market, even mediocre salespeople survive. Like the ant vs. the grasshopper fable, though, don't just kick back and expect winter will never come. The next downturn is always around the corner—it's a sales cycle, and you need to be prepared. After all, you don't want to be mediocre, and you certainly don't want to become extinct.

I encourage you to be one of the 20% who will empower themselves and thrive after the current sales evolution, *not* the 80% who will find themselves jobless because they turned a blind eye.

Section 1:

What's Going on Out There?

Don't Become Extinct!

Can It Really Be All That Bad?

If you're a sales veteran, you've probably been through a number of sales cycles. You've had ups and downs, you've ridden out the storms, and you know that ultimately, things return to normal. You start hitting your numbers again, and all is right with the world.

This time, though, nothing will return to "normal." There is only change, restructuring, and finding new tools to help you survive if you're lucky, and thrive if you're good.

Buyers are changing all the rules of engagement, and they will never go back to the way they used to conduct business with you. Granted, you may have a few long-time customers who will stick with you no matter what, but when it comes to prospecting and adding new buyers to the mix, all bets are off.

Buyers are redefining what they will accept as far as your prospecting efforts go. They hold tremendous power, thanks to the internet and technology. They're more informed than ever, and they don't need you as much as they used to. In some industries, they may now be able to bypass you altogether and make their purchases entirely online.

What benefit do you offer, then, either to your employer or your prospects? Ahhh, there's the million-dollar question. We will explore solutions to help you maintain your value, but first, we need to look at the different aspects of the shifts in buyer behavior that are afoot.

Throughout this book, I'll share with you my findings of a recent buyer survey. This pie chart shows you the wide-ranging composition of the survey participants:

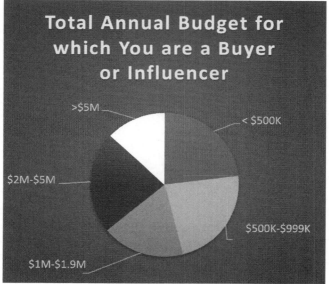

Source: Shawna Suckow International

Don't Become Extinct!

The Shift in How Buyers Buy

Our culture has changed buyers everywhere. Everyone's a customer to some degree. You're a customer. Your buying habits have changed, haven't they? The way that you expect to be "sold to" has changed.

Think about how you would go about purchasing a car today. Where do you begin your research?

When I was a young girl, my father and I would go visit car lots to do preliminary research. Today, your research begins long before you ever step foot onto a car lot. You're armed with all sorts of information, including what other customers have paid for that model. You've talked with friends and family, and checked out the rankings given by complete strangers about the car model in question. You've located all the features, both standard and optional, and have learned the safety ratings as well. Only then do you step onto the car lot and actually speak to a salesperson. In fact, you can even skip that step and buy a car before ever stepping onto the car lot.

Clearly, you're a savvier consumer than my father was decades ago. You're more knowledgeable about your purchases, you don't have to wait to be educated by a salesperson, you know as much about their competitors as they do, and you don't have to accept the information they give you as the hard truth.

You have changed as a consumer. You have become more immune to traditional sales techniques, you can find the information you need without a middleman, and you have no qualms about buying direct without involving a salesperson. By the same token, boy have your target buyers changed, too.

When the economy took its most recent downturn, we started closing ourselves off to all of the things that, out of politeness' sake, we used to be open to. Prior to then, we would pick up the phone if somebody was calling us at work, because it was the polite thing to do.

I bet you don't get many people answering your cold calls these days. In fact, my research shows that if you make 100 cold calls, 96 go to voice mail. You're being largely ignored, and you know there must be a better way.

Back in the day, if someone left a voice mail message, we'd at least occasionally return the call, even if to politely say, "No thanks." Today, as you well know, leave a voice mail message and you'll be lucky to hear back from one or two out of 100 of those buyers.

That means that the overwhelming majority of your cold calling time is wasted. Rest assured, there is a better way, and it's called The Trifecta. I discuss it in detail in Section 4.

Email Losing Effectiveness

Before the recession, we were more responsive to emails than we are today. We'd at least respond with a polite "thanks but no thanks;" whereas today, we just ignore and delete them without so much as a reply—much like voice mail.

Now that emails are largely read on mobile devices versus computers, it's even easier for your prospects to hit that delete button, without even previewing your message. In this age of media saturation, we've all become extremely quick to judge anything or anyone attempting to sell something to us.

What happened during the recession to make us so jaded?

It was a perfect storm, so to speak.

Especially in the U.S., with the downturn in the economy, buyers didn't have the bandwidth pay attention to all the marketing messages. We were just hyper-focused on the task at hand, and getting through the day. Very likely, if we still had a job, we were in a department that was severely downsized, and we were just trying to get all the work done and stay employed.

Around that same time, salespeople everywhere were getting more and more aggressive because buyers were getting less and less responsive. The salespeople started doubling and tripling their calling and emailing, while their buyers were redoubling their efforts to ignore all the noise and just get their tasks done. Sales efforts went up, buyer responsiveness went down. You simply became easier to ignore.

Because buyers had less time to focus on the process of buying, they looked for ways to speed up the process, and many turned to technology. In some cases, this meant circumventing salespeople altogether, to avoid the time-consuming phone calls, emails and visits. To make the process easier and quicker, rather than doing full due diligence with a salesperson, buyers simply turned to other resources for information that salespeople used to provide—namely, buyers turned to their peers, social media, and Google.

You simply became easier to ignore.

Salespeople used to play a key role during the research phase of a purchase, but those days were ending. Why turn to a stranger who has skin in the game, when your peers are unbiased? Why slow down your buying process to wait for a salesperson to call you back, return your email, or meet with you, when you can Google in your pajamas and get the features and benefits of the product or service online and at your convenience? Salespeople became an inconvenient middleman in the new era of expedience.

Buyers also turned to message boards, LinkedIn groups, and Facebook communities of their peers to get straight answers. Keep in mind, these "peers" can be complete strangers—they simply have to have something in common—age, gender, industry, geography, or simply a common interest in a product.

We've all seen those posts: "Has anyone tried SalesForce? Stayed at the Omni Shoreham? Tried Expensify? Bought the new Apple product?" Strangers are more than happy to help each other with unbiased (from a sales perspective, at least) feedback and suggestions.

The result: the "how" of buying evolved and salespeople became a commodity in the eyes of many buyers.

Don't Become Extinct!

The Shift in When Buyers Buy

With the rise of the printed catalog back in the last century, a lot of door-to-door salespeople lost their jobs. That was the first major shift in consumer behavior since the trading post.

Then, along came the internet, which caused the second major shift in consumer behavior. A lot more salespeople lost their jobs, especially in the retail arena where many brick-and-mortar stores either died (Blockbuster, anyone?), evolved into hybrid models (Target and Target.com), or were entirely replaced by retail game-changers (Amazon.com).

The third wave of sales evolution will be in the B2B arena. Consumers have become comfortable doing their retail shopping from home. Many of those consumers are B2B buyers at work, so it should come as no surprise that they seek out the same conveniences, and are savvier in their methods.

The result: A growing number of B2B buyers no longer need salespeople early in the process for information gathering.

Salespeople are coming into the transaction later than ever before—when the buyer is ready, or almost ready, to buy.

This is a game-changer!

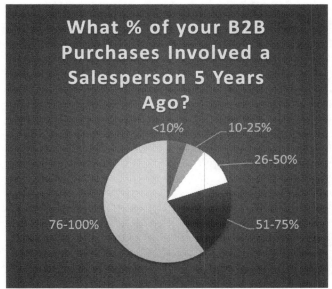

What % of your B2B
Purchases Involved a
Salesperson 5 Years
Ago?

<10%   10-25%

26-50%

76-100%   51-75%

Source: Shawna Suckow International

Compare the previous chart with this one, and observe the obvious shift in buyer behavior taking place. Buyers are clearly relying less and less on salespeople to help them through the transaction process. This is the foundation for this entire book—your fight to stay relevant amidst shifting buyer behavior.

Source: Shawna Suckow International

The buyer is coming to you more informed than ever, with a pre-determined opinion of your product or service, and full knowledge of your competition as well. They probably know your Unique Selling Proposition (USP) as well as you do.

Buyers are certainly savvier than ever before. They're entering the sales funnel later than ever before. Your job is no longer about informing the buyer. By the time they reach out to you, they're probably ready to buy.

This is quite an interesting shift.

Your job used to have four main components.

1. Prospect and build relationships.
2. Ensure the buyer understands your product/service and your Unique Selling Proposition.
3. Help the buyer enter the sales funnel.
4. Close the deal at the best possible terms for your company.

Today, the buyer evolution is eliminating and changing these components.

- It's more important than ever for you to prospect and build relationships, but buyers are resisting your efforts more than ever before.
- As a result, your company's marketing team bears the brunt of building awareness today. They're struggling to reach buyers as well, because of the saturation

of media messaging constantly bombarding us. Buyers are becoming experts at tuning out all types of sales and marketing messages *until they're ready to buy*.

- You can't force a buyer into a sales funnel today—they can smell it a mile away, and will resist your efforts. If you're too aggressive or too easy to circumvent, they'll seek out ways to make their purchases without you.
- Closing deals on the best possible terms for your company has gradually gotten more difficult, as buyers are more informed than ever about what things should cost, and the best time of year to make purchases.

In summary, buyers are waiting until they're darn good and ready to pull the trigger, and that's impacting every component of the traditional sales funnel. You may not even know they're lurking out there until the deal is practically ready to close.

That's how the "when" of buying has evolved.

Don't Become Extinct!

The Shift in Why Buyers Buy

Buyers make purchases because there's a need—that much is obvious. What I'm proposing is that there's been a shift in why buyers buy from salespeople when there are alternate ways to make a purchase.

Today, there are certainly more convenient ways to make most purchases than the old-fashioned method of talking to a salesperson from start to finish.

In 2015, online shopping surpassed in-person shopping on Black Friday for the first time in history. Why? When the buying experience becomes a hassle, customers look for alternatives. Companies that provide alternatives are succeeding, and it's having repercussions on sales jobs (again, example: Amazon.com).

Remember when Zappos first came to market? My first reaction was, "How can I buy shoes on-line without trying them on?" Today, I buy plenty of shoes, and most everything else, online whenever I can. The physical store only wins out when a) I can't wait for shipping, b) when I need something I can't acquire online, or c) when I just want the experience of going to the mall (which is extremely rare these days—and I live near the biggest mall in America).

It's no different for B2B buyers. The physical interaction with a real, live salesperson wins out only when:
- the buyer can't acquire the information/product/service any other way,
- working with you cuts down on the time or effort to complete the transaction, or
- the buyer has a relationship and wants the experience of interacting with you.

Do you see where I'm going with this? Your role is weakening in the buyer's world and you're getting circumvented more and more. Unless you build those relationships, buyers will choose the convenience of going online more and more.

I remember a coaching session with a businessperson who sells high-end signs for conventions. His signs were patented, unique in that they were completely reusable given their design, and extremely durable so they would last several years. The typical alternative was a highly delicate sign that could be typically used only once, and then went to the landfill. The company certainly had a corner on the high-end signage market and the green/sustainability market in their product niche.

As I assessed the business website, I noticed that there was no way for buyers to order online. When I asked him why, he replied that he preferred his customers talk to a salesperson. "Well," I asked, "What about what your customers prefer?" His customers are busy planners who deal with thousands of details for a convention, and they want to be able to order commodities like signs and name badges with ease. He was creating an unnecessary barrier between his customers and his products.

By putting his products online, would the result be an elimination of his sales team? Not necessarily. The product was not well known in the industry, so his team still played a key role in prospecting, educating, and relationship-building. When the time came for a planner to order signs, those salespeople could ensure the order would come to their company. They would no longer be inbound sales reps fielding inquiries—they would become much more strategic, and, therefore, important to the company's bottom line.

Are you being strategic? Are you prospecting and keeping the pipeline full? Or, are you standing in the way of a great solution to keep your buyers happy and maintain your relevance?

If you're not focusing the majority of your time on prospecting and relationship-building today, your years as a salesperson are most certainly numbered.

It then comes down to this: How can you prospect and build relationships with buyers today, when they seem determined to keep salespeople at arm's length?

I'm glad you asked. Read on for solutions that really work.

Don't Become Extinct!

The Shift in Where Buyers Buy

T hanks to FedEx and the fax machine, buyers haven't had to meet face-to-face to make a purchase in decades. The fax has thankfully been replaced by email and sharing documents via "the cloud." These are just two more examples of how the sales process has evolved over the years.

Thanks to our multitude of devices, we can make major purchasing decisions and sign contracts from home in our pajamas, or from Basecamp at Mount Everest (not sure who would want to, but it's at least possible).

If buyers are changing *where* they make purchasing decisions, along

with *how*, *when*, and *why*, then clearly,
the next phase of buyer evolution is
already happening.

The (Ugh) Paradigm Shift

Although I hate the term, there's truly been a "paradigm shift" in the way buyers are letting you into their world to start the sales process.

There are new ways to approach your buyers. There are better methods to employ when putting your products or services out there. I'm going to get into greater detail and give you some solutions that are actually working, because I know that what you've been doing is not working the way that it used to five or 10 years ago. It's not working now, and the world is not suddenly going to go back to the way it was. Your buyers are evolving!

I hate hearing a salesperson beat himself up, saying he just needs to work harder, because of the old adage, "It's a numbers game." It isn't about working harder; it's about harnessing the powerful tools that will help you work smarter.

Section 2:

How Salespeople Can Adapt

Don't Become Extinct!

Your Marketing Efforts: More Important Than Ever

This much hasn't changed: When buyers are researching, you want to be the one they find most appealing, so that when they're ready to buy, they think of you first and foremost.

You might think marketing should be left to the marketing department. In the current era though, individuals at every level of the company play a role in marketing, thanks to social media. We all have a social media footprint—whether yours leads your customers to you or repels them is up to you.

Everything you do on social media as an individual, therefore, needs to be either completely private or customer supportive. If you want to post things you don't want your customers to see, then make sure your social profiles (Facebook, Instagram, etc.) are private. Otherwise, every post you make is part of your very public social profile—and you need to be cognizant of that.

Blurring Lines Between Customers and Friends

Another marked shift in buyer behavior is the blurring of social lines. As I mentioned previously, buyers buy from people they like. It's a natural progression these days for buyers to want to become part of your social circle—if you're doing your job correctly. Why? Because customers want to see you as a peer, and once you reach peer status, you become a trusted part of their inner circle, and that means their social media circle.

Many salespeople, especially older generations, are uncomfortable with this blurring of lines. They want to keep a separation between their business and personal lives. That's your prerogative, but be wary of offending your customers by turning down their Facebook and other social requests.

An outdated solution was to create separate Facebook profiles for your business self and your private self. This isn't necessary anymore, since Facebook and others now allow you to create separate circles and privacy settings depending on who you want seeing your posts. You now can create divisions for family, close friends, business colleagues, ex-boyfriends, whatever you like! Then when you post something a little too personal for your customers, you simply don't share it with that circle.

Prospecting:
More Important Than Ever

As a salesperson, know this: Your initial contact with the buyer has become less about *giving* information, and more about *getting* it. Your buyer has online access to most of the information you could possibly offer as a salesperson, so your role as an educator is diminished.

Your role has shifted to acquiring information about your customer, as that becomes harder and harder to come by. I'm not talking about company information you can find online, I'm talking about challenges and motivations of that individual within her company. The more information you can collect during the initial (and possibly only) contact is critical to your follow-up.

This is why the most pivotal role you can play today as a salesperson is that of prospector.

Every other role you play has been compromised or minimized by the buyer. If you don't get in early—way before the buyer is ready to buy—you no longer stand much of a chance anymore of influencing the buyer.

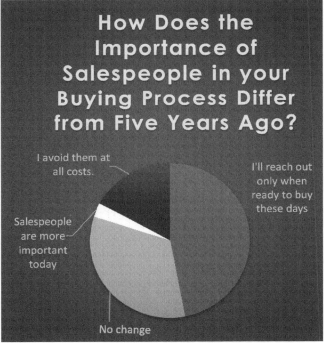

Source: Shawna Suckow International

Have you ever received a Request For Proposal (RFP), but you had a sneaking suspicion the buyer had already decided to go with another seller? Your intuition is probably right. The buyer is going with an existing relationship with some other salesperson, or the buyer has already researched and found her solution, and is now just following protocol.

That's why prospecting is so critical. It's about teeing up relationships much earlier than before, so that when buyers are ready, they think not just of your company, but of you.

By the time the buyer reaches out to a salesperson these days, the majority of the buying decision has been made. The buyer already has her top choice in mind, and may be reaching out to you to:

1) help her reinforce her decision to buy from you,
2) help her build her case with her boss why *not* to buy from you, or
3) she's already decided to buy from you but is looking to negotiate. You have very little influence at this stage, especially if you have no prior relationship. Relationships do matter,

and if you haven't formed one before the RFP stage, or before the buyer reaches out to you the first time, you're probably too late. The buying process moves too quickly these days for you to form any meaningful relationship once the buyer is ready to buy. The cards simply fall where they may.

At this stage of buyer evolution, you're on the brink of extinction for two reasons:

1) You've become an order-taker, not a value-adder, and as soon as the buyer can eliminate you from the process, she will.
2) You can easily be replaced by an administrative person if you're just processing inbound orders.

That's why you have to up your prospecting game! You've got to reverse the buyer trend toward eliminating you, and inject yourself into the process by building relationships far and wide, so that the buyer wants you involved.

This happens when the buyer sees you as an advocate and an ally, which only happens if there's a relationship. Otherwise, he sees you as an adversary or a hurdle.

This is another huge shift in today's buyer mentality and your role as a salesperson.

You must rethink your role: You're no longer an advocate of your company, you're an advocate of your customer.

When you can truly embrace this mindset, you are ready for the future of buyer evolution. Trust me, when you embody this, buyers can sense it. When you don't, buyers can sense it even more (which is another reason why buyers avoid salespeople!).

How can you become a better advocate for your customers? Write some ideas below.

1. _____

_____

2. _____

_____

3. _____

_____

Don't Become Extinct!

Listening: One of the Most Important Sales Skills

There's an undercurrent of buyer dissatisfaction out there, so I think it's time for a killer reminder of what today's customers really want in a transaction.

Even though we are ultimately going to buy a product or service, it's not really about that. It's not about the extra features, either. It's not about the price.

All our conversations, negotiations, and ruminations are about what we are trying to *achieve*, not what we're trying to buy.

When we say we want to replace an antiquated Customer Relationship Management (CRM) system, for example, we aren't saying we want you to talk our ears off about your product, and its features (this is what your competitors do, so take a different approach).

Ask us what we are trying to achieve with a new CRM system and listen carefully to the answer. We don't really want a new system simply because the existing system is old. We may say we want to be more efficient, and we want Betty, the office assistant with no computer skills, to be able to navigate the system easily.

These are specific goals and it's all-too-commonplace for most salespeople to insert their pitch about features like a simple weekly report being only two clicks away, and the free training you can offer for Betty. However, you're no ordinary salesperson, so you know that this is only addressing specific goals, and it is not what we ultimately want to achieve.

Try asking again. Ask us what we want to achieve by having more efficient communications and by bringing Betty into the new millennium. At this point, we'll probably have an answer that better resembles what we are *actually* looking for.

We may say we want to grow and expand our business. This type of answer is where things get interesting. Now you can tell us about your brand's success rate and soothe our concerns about expanding in our competitive market.

We will (half-heartedly) listen to features and product descriptions, but that's not what we want from you (we can get that from Google).

We will be glad to know you are willing to address our specific goals, but, address *what we are trying to achieve* and our ears will perk up. You will have surpassed simple conversations on products and services, and surpassed the point at which your competition feels they've done their job. Help us achieve a vision and you'll not only make the sale, you'll also have a lifelong customer.

Think of a current prospect and picture your conversation. What are three fact-finding questions you can ask to better understand their real goals?

1. _____

_____

2. _____

_____

3. _____

_____

The Sales Funnel is Starting Later & Later

Buyers are entering the sales funnel later than ever before. Why? Because buyers are self-educating these days, and their first contact with your company may not be until they're actually ready to buy. Salespeople are having a harder time cultivating customers these days, because buyers are resisting traditional sales efforts.

This has two implications for salespeople.

1. With buyers self-educating, you need to make sure you and your brand are out there and easy to find when buyers are searching. It's not just the job of your marketing department anymore. Later in this book, you'll find an arsenal of tools that actually work

today, to make your life a lot easier.

2. Salespeople have to be prepared to interact with buyers who are much further down the purchasing road than in previous years. You're probably getting a lot more contact from buyers who have already narrowed down their list, are well informed about your product or service, and are ready (or almost ready) to be closed.

You'll have to be more savvy at determining where the buyer is in the process, and why they need you at this point. This means *not* jumping into your usual routine of educating the buyer by listing off features and benefits, as this will be borderline insulting—they already know more about your company than you might think.

Ask the buyer the right questions and truly listen. They already know their problem and see your company as a solution, so no need to go into the nitty-gritty. Treat them as the well-informed, savvy buyer they are. Get to the meat of it—if they can bypass you in their purchasing but they haven't, what do they need that you can offer? Why are they truly contacting you?

How can you phrase three questions to help you sleuth out why the buyer is really contacting you?

1. _____

_____

2. _____

_____

3. _____

_____

Don't Become Extinct!

What's Not Working Today

What's the definition of insanity? Doing the same thing over and over again and expecting different results.

What's the definition of Insanity 2.0? Doing the same thing you used to do five or 10 years ago, and expecting the whole world to go back to the way things used to be! That is not going to happen.

I know many of you have bosses who simply don't get it. They're living in the past, because they haven't been in a customer-facing role in years (or decades!). They're giving you outdated advice, and measuring you on metrics that no longer work on today's evolving buyers.

Let's start with what's not working.

NOTE: If you're running a sales department and you've found this book on your desk with this section bookmarked and highlighted, you've got some pretty frustrated salespeople! Empower them by unleashing their true skills that *will* work in today's market.

What are some sales methods that no longer work for you?

1. _____

_____

2. _____

_____

3. _____

_____

Cold Calling

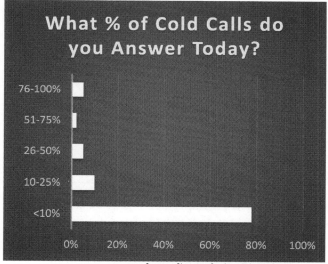

What % of Cold Calls do you Answer Today?

Source: Shawna Suckow International

The way you need to prospect today is completely different, and it will not revert back to the good ol' days. As a salesperson, you know this. You've sensed this change coming for years, and your traditional sales efforts, cold calling first and foremost, are hitting a lot of brick walls.

We are not suddenly going to go back to using fax machines, for example. None of us is suddenly going to start picking up the phone again. We have trained ourselves not to do that anymore. We're far more efficient and greedy with our time than to give it to a stranger who isn't on our appointment calendar already.

I know many of you are still required to make cold calls, and I'm sorry. Don't give up, though, because you'll soon learn about The Trifecta process later in this book. It's another way you can still use the phone, but in a stronger, more productive way.

Bad Email Tactics

Let me ask you: How many emails do you get in a single day? How many do you ignore and delete without a thought? I would guess conservatively that 70% of the emails you receive don't get your time or attention, just deleted.

B2B buyers are no different, but the volume of emails we get is staggering. Salespeople know we don't answer the phone, so they're emailing us. A lot.

Some buyers will still save the occasional email to a folder for later. Even fewer will bother to respond. Most of us simply delete them, figuring that when we're ready to buy, we don't need to dig through an email folder, we'll just use Google, social media, and peers to begin our research process.

Heard of Sanebox or Unroll.me? These are just a couple of the tools that are weeding out cold emails— especially email blasts—from buyer inboxes like never before. Moreover, with these tools, buyers can easily remove themselves from your list with one click, so using bulk email incorrectly can whittle your list down to nothing.

In short, buyers have trained themselves not to respond to your emails anymore. We have to decide what we can afford to spare the time on, and what <u>matters</u>. We're just like you with your email inbox, we're merciless.

You have to matter, and in order to matter, you have to become part of our trusted inner circle.

Overt Salesyness

You'll see me use the word 'salesy' a lot in this book, and it might not be a real word. It definitely has the right connotation that I'm going for. You know the used-car salesman feel? That's overt salesyness. It's the guy who's after a quick buck. He's slick, he uses big words, and he never quite listens to what you are saying. He's the guy that is working the room at a party, and during your conversation, he's already looking around to land his next client.

It hopefully goes without saying, but this is the type of behavior that makes everyone say "ewwww" these days. While the above example is a bit laughable, I bet you know someone who's like this!

Most salespeople today are just decent people trying to build relationships, do their job, and feed their family. There are still quite a few behaviors that are turnoffs to your prospects though, and you might not even be aware that you're doing some of them.

Buyers are ultra-sensitive these days to salesyness. They're not interested in what I call the "hit and run" sales tactics. In fact, you may be surprised what they value most in a salesperson.

The top two characteristics (#1 Reliable and Responsive, and #2 Trustworthy) are probably of the same importance as they were 20 or 30 years ago. The big shift comes in the characteristics that rank next.

#3 in overall importance, behind the obvious 'reliability' and 'trustworthiness,' is someone who is authentic and non-salesy! Buyers place a huge value on that these days, and that's a big shift. In fact, it's more important to buyers than understanding their business!

Authenticity means being real, flawed, and generally human. If you're going for perfect, you're missing the point. Showing a little humanity goes a long way today.

Don't Become Extinct!

Section 3:

What *Is* Working Today

Don't Become Extinct!

Let's begin with the new paradigm in selling, so that you have a strong foundation in exactly what's working in sales theory, and then we'll move into specific tools.

S.P.A.D.E.S.

This is an important acronym because it represents the most important shifts in what buyers are expecting today.

Social Proof

The first 'S' in S.P.A.D.E.S. stands for Social Proof. When your customers endorse you to other customers, it's the most valuable marketing you can have. That's the foundation of *Social Proof*.

Buyers don't automatically trust or believe you anymore, because you have skin in the game, so to speak. This is where Social Proof becomes so important – it's the most trusted form of marketing available to you.

Let me share an alarming statistic to illustrate this point. According to *AdAge*, back in 2008, 77% of buyers suddenly started distrusting businesses! That's the shift that happened when the economy took a downturn. Three-fourths of us—consumers of all kinds—just flipped a switch between 2008 and 2009, deciding, "I don't trust your business anymore. I'm going to trust my peers and what my peers say about you, before I trust what *you* say about your company." Even if those peers are complete strangers!

Fellow travelers on TripAdvisor.com, for example, are deemed more trustworthy than the hotels marketing to travelers, even though those travelers are complete strangers. They're more trustworthy because they're not trying to sell anything—they're simply trying to be helpful.

We all collectively as a culture now rely on our peers' opinions more than any other source. If you can harness your current customers' willingness to tell your story, that's the golden ticket.

The bottom line: People don't trust businesses anymore; they trust other people.

Social Proof is what other people say about your company (or about you as a salesperson). Gathering Social Proof is becoming more and more critical going forward, because without it, 77% of buyers immediately distrust you and your company.

Your mission then is to proactively start capturing positive things others are saying about you and your company, and share those in your sales & marketing efforts.

Show them what others say about you—collect it, organize it, and make it easy for the buyer to find.

How do you do that? Let me begin by telling you buyers no longer trust written testimonials on your website or in your proposals. They've moved on, like the rest of the world, to video. Video has more credibility and more dimension to it. You can look in someone's eyes and immediately determine if you trust what they're saying. Written testimonials are too easily manipulated, or outright faked.

So whenever you have a happy buyer—whether you're a commercial real estate broker, a convention center salesperson, or an international exporter—make an effort to collect social proof in the form of video.

This can mean simply grabbing your smartphone or tablet and asking the buyer for a quick video testimonial. Here are some notes on video testimonials.

- Catch the buyer when they've just thanked you and they're happy with the transaction. Don't give them a chance to think it over—most will overthink it and the video will seem scripted. Just ask them to share one or two sentences about you, your company, or the transaction into your phone.
- Ask the buyer for permission to use the video on your website, on YouTube, etc. If your lawyers are uncomfortable with this, you may need a signed release. I've never used this, but you might need to.
- You may think you need a high-quality film crew and backdrop, but you don't. Of course, you can go to that effort and expense, but buyers trust the raw, shaky footage on a smartphone more than they trust a big production with perfect lighting and what could easily be actors.

- If your buyer isn't local, ask them for a Skype call to follow up. If they say nice things, ask them if you can record the video call.

The point is to proactively capture your happy customers saying complimentary things about you and the transaction, for the benefit of future buyers. Nothing will make your other prospects more comfortable quicker than hearing from their peers that everything was great.

As a professional speaker and sales trainer, whenever I have audience members come up and compliment me afterward, I try to collect one or two video testimonials. I add these to my YouTube channel, along with other videos I've created on sales tips, etc. That way, my channel is constantly kept fresh with new content, and over the years I've collected a lot of Social Proof for any prospects considering hiring me. I simply direct prospects to my channel, and let them see what other people say about me, rather than try to convey how great I am to them (that seems disingenuous).

People

The second letter of S.P.A.D.E.S. stands for People. People don't trust businesses anymore; we've already established that. They trust other people. That means that you have to start telling the story of the people within your company, and the people who buy from you. It means conveying your message to prospects using real stories, not facts, figures, features, or benefits.

There are huge benefits to telling, rather than selling. According to Prevention Magazine (Sept 2016), "What engages your brain more than music or math? University of California, Berkeley, researchers have discovered that it's storytelling. Their studies show that listening to story podcasts activated sensations, emotions, and memories not just on one side but across the entire brain, thereby upending right brain/left brain theory."

What this means is that in order to be your most memorable self (something every salesperson strives for with prospects), engage your customers by telling them stories about your product, your service, or how you solved a problem for another customer. That makes you far more memorable than your competition, who simply tells the prospect how great he is at solving problems.

Here are three starter stories you can formulate to share with prospects:

1. I once solved this problem for a customer:

2. I got into this business because I'm passionate about:

3. I want to tell you about my co-worker, _____. He/she did this amazing thing for a customer once:

There are several ways you can share stories with prospects. The best is always face-to-face, whether that be in person, or via Skype. If you can't get facetime with a prospect, share videos you've recorded of customers talking about you, your team, and your product/service.

List three customers who would happily give you a video testimonial today:

1.

2.

3.

Authenticity

The "A" in S.P.A.D.E.S. stands for Authenticity, which has become hugely important to buyers. They don't want to buy from someone who is salesy, stale, or stand-offish. People buy from people they like!

This may seem obvious, but it's amazingly under-appreciated. Salespeople still think they need to be uber-professional, when, in fact, buyers today want to do business with someone who's a regular, relatable person. They want to work with people who feel like part of their circle—part of their community.

So how do you become part of our community? You have to slow down to speed up. I know that sounds crazy, but you will sell more by being less salesy.

You can't just hit us with sales message after sales message, all written in "marketing-speak" with big words and lists of benefits. I ignore those and delete those—they don't resonate with me for even a second.

You have to be authentic. You have to be approachable. You have to be human. You have to be flawed. The perfectly coiffed sales guy with the perfectly polished shoes and the glossy brochures isn't any of those things to us anymore—except untrustworthy right off the bat.

> *Authentic.*
> *Approachable. Flawed.*
> *Human. It bears*
> *repeating and paying*
> *special attention to*
> *now more than ever.*

Authentic.

You have to be authentic to me, meaning be a real person first, salesperson second, and company third. You have to come at me with different sales messages that are wrapped in authenticity. Don't spew features and benefits! Everybody's volume of emails has doubled or tripled over the past five years. I can't tell you how many salespeople's messages sound exactly the same as everybody else's!

You all have the best service, the best prices, the best products, the best this, the best that. When everybody is saying they're the best, we can't trust any of them! We cannot differentiate that. And we no longer believe it when coming from a salesperson.

Approachable.

Being approachable means being a real person, talking like a real person, and having a normal conversation not peppered with closing questions. Establish the relationship first—just back down and don't seem desperate to close the sale. You have to woo us more these days.

Flawed.

Even Superman has his Kryptonite. Don't try to come off as perfect—we can smell a rat and you're not doing yourself any favors. Tell us what's *not* perfect about what you're selling! That's the type of thing that builds trust.

Human.

For God's sake, be a human being to us. Let us get to know you as a person first. Talk about your kids, your vacation, your flat tire. Then you can move toward your role as a salesperson. Think of it like dating—you don't try to make a move before we chit chat and establish some sort of rapport, right? We want to work with the person who makes us feel comfortable, now more than ever. What's likeable about you as a person? Show us that.

> How can you be more authentic in your written communications going forward? (Hint: a great place to start is your LinkedIn profile)

Differentiation

The "D" in S.P.A.D.E.S. stands for
Differentiation. As I mentioned before,
buyers everywhere (yourself included)
are overly marketed to, and we've
trained ourselves to ignore sales
messages and advertisements.

More than ever, this means you
have to stand out, or risk being ignored.
Catch their attention, or be deleted in
less time than it took for you to hit
"send." You have to have a different
message, and tell it in a different way—
both in person and online.

---

*Does your marketing
pass the "No, really?"
test?*

What do I mean by that?
Differentiation is saying things that are
not typical and not expected among all
your competitors, and not in your
brochure. "We have great service."

"No, really? I expect you to say that and frankly everyone says that, so I just don't believe it.

"We have the best widget." No, really? That's exactly what your direct competitors say. When everyone claims to be the best, everyone but one of you is lying, because only one of you truly IS the best. Do you see how all this traditional marketing-speak is really just talk with no substance anymore?

Tell me how you're going to NOT be a pain in my butt, how you're going to make my life 172% easier, how your product is going to make me not pull out my hair.

Use some humor. Catch me off-guard. Make me curious. But DON'T tell me you have the best widget. Puh-lease.

I learned this the hard way because with the professional association I founded, I was trying to sell to senior-level buyers all the time. About five years ago, I decided our marketing needed an overhaul to be much more professional. Before that time, we were a robust, growing, upstart association that didn't take ourselves too seriously.

I re-wrote everything on our web site. Our Unique Selling Proposition, our sales messages, our membership information – all of it was revised to be ultra-professional and use all the latest buzz-words. I thought we had to aspire to be more like the biggest professional associations out there, and that's how they sounded.

Boy, was I wrong.

Today, we've revamped all our messaging to go back to our original instincts – to be human, authentic, and real. NOT ultra-professional, claiming to be the best this or that. Now, we connect with people on a human level, using authentic verbiage and just talking to them through the pages of our web site. The results are astounding

– far more new members are attracted to us because they believe what we're saying. We don't sound like the competition, we sound like "us" and it's attractive.

If you're using any of your industry's overused buzz-words, go back and rethink what you're saying. Rethink your brochures, your emails, your conversations. Trust me – your buyers aren't believing any of the hype and overused terminology.

I know many of you aren't going to have the ability to change your website if you work for a big company. But change, remove all of these words as much as you can from your emails, from your blog, from your proposals - whatever you do have control over.

A Differentiation Case Study

Let me tell you about my friend, Greg. He's a salesperson, but he doesn't behave that way. I asked him about his sales philosophy once, and he said, "I don't attempt to sell anything to anyone until I've helped that person twice."

When Greg first meets you, he listens to you. He asks questions and determines what you need. Whether that's an introduction to someone, a link to an on-line article, or a drink after a long day, he selflessly does whatever he can to help you. Twice. Only then will he broach a sales conversation.

I think this is brilliant—he builds rapport, and lays the foundation for a true friendship by being selfless. He doesn't shove his business card at you and tell you about how fabulous his products are, and that he'll follow up with you on Monday. Nope, Greg has realized what many salespeople are still learning: If you make it about the buyer first, the buyer will let you into her community and consider you a peer who's trustworthy and helpful.

Remember what I said about buyers no longer trusting companies or salespeople? They trust their peers. Your best strategy is to work toward becoming a peer and a resource. If you focus on the one-off sale (what I call the "hit and run"), you'll soon face extinction.

Education

Now that you're working toward becoming a trusted peer and resource to your prospects, that means less selling and more educating. You can't do this effectively unless you know what keeps your prospects up at night. Once you learn that secret, you can effectively educate.

This means sending your prospects articles written by independent parties—scientists, professors, industry experts—whose messages educate your buyers. It means inviting your prospects to seminars or webinars put on by third parties.

Anything you can do to educate without overtly selling will build trust in you as a resource and distance you from being an untrusted company or salesperson.

Who are your top three competitors?

1.

2.

3.

Research them on-line and see how they are positioning themselves. How can you differentiate yourself? Write some ideas below.

Solutions

The last letter in S.P.A.D.E.S. is for solutions. If you don't know what your prospects are losing sleep over, then you can't provide specific solutions.

It comes down to research. If you haven't met the prospect yet, use the internet to gain as much intelligence as you can, before you reach out. This is critical, because an overly general email or phone call is easily ignored. A specific one that shows you are concerned with what the buyer or her company are going through is far more impressive.

If you have an existing relationship with the prospect, a face-to-face meeting is always best, but I know that's getting more and more difficult as buyers protect their calendars like never before.

If you meet in person, say, at a cocktail party, let the buyer do most of the talking. I cannot overemphasize this! It's a rare opportunity to gain intelligence straight from the buyer's mouth, so don't waste it.

Let me tell you a story about my friend Kris, who is a salesperson. She was at a tradeshow, and sat down at a community lunch table for a quick bite. A woman sat down next to her, and she turned out to be a hugely important prospect. Rather than kick into sales mode, Kris made friendly conversation and asked the woman about herself, her company, and her challenges.

Meanwhile, another salesperson came over, sat down, and introduced herself. Upon seeing the buyer's nametag, the salesperson immediately went into a huge sales pitch, did most of the talking, finished her sandwich, left her business card, and exited the scene.

The buyer sighed loudly, and my friend Kris said, "I bet you get that a lot." They had a good laugh, and continued their conversation. At the end of their meal, the buyer noticed who Kris was with, and was immediately taken aback. Kris's company competed directly with that of the obnoxious salesperson. The buyer gave Kris her card, and thanked her profusely for the nice, non-salesy conversation.

Kris sent her a fun follow-up message, and today this buyer is one of Kris's largest accounts.

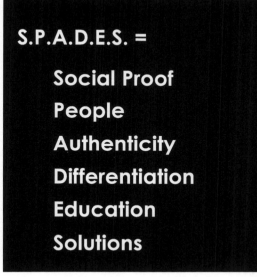

S.P.A.D.E.S. =

Social Proof
People
Authenticity
Differentiation
Education
Solutions

Don't Become Extinct!

How Do Prospects Prefer to be Contacted Today?

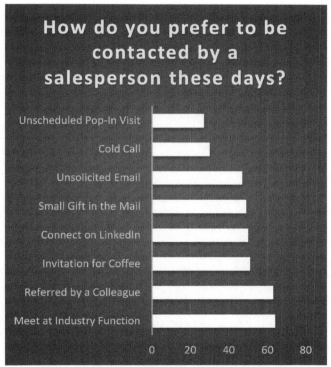

Source: Shawna Suckow International

Each of these holds an important key for you in building new relationships today. Dig in to this next section, because these tips come straight from buyers!

Industry Networking

Clearly, buyers prefer to meet salespeople face-to-face, in a low-pressure environment, such as at an industry function. It's the No. 1 way buyers want to meet you, so it's more important than ever to show up! It's how you behave when you show up that will make all the difference today. Everyone hates to be "sold at." If you're trying to close a deal over a cocktail with someone you just met, you may need to rethink your methods.

This chance meeting may be your only opportunity to gain information on your buyer, so spend it wisely! Show interest and listen 90% of the time. It's like a first date—don't be pushy or talk about yourself the whole time. What a turnoff!

Referrals 2.0

The second-most preferred way buyers want to meet you is via referral from a trusted colleague. Referrals are so important in the era of buyer evolution, because you've already passed the peer test. That's a huge hurdle! Buyers trust their peers more than ever before, so an endorsement from a current customer is worth its weight in gold.

Referrals 1.0 were easy—they fell in your lap, and you didn't have to do much to cultivate them. Today, with referrals being more important than ever, you have to be strategic. That's Referrals 2.0.

My 20-60-20 Rule

Do you have a plan in place to solicit referrals from active clients? If so, I hope it's more than a satisfaction survey you send out after the transaction. You need to motivate and encourage clients to refer their friends, because of my 20-60-20 rule. I'll explain...

About 20% of your clients are rabid fans of you and/or your company. They are active ambassadors, spreading the word about your greatness without you having to take much action (if any). They give you five stars on customer feedback sites. They share your name with friends and family. They are the ones most likely to Friend you on Facebook. They may even send *you* a holiday card!

And, 60% of your clients are generally happy with you, but won't take further action to refer you without some effort on your part.

The remaining 20% of your clients will never refer you, never take action, and never become ambassadors, for a variety of reasons (ambivalence, lack of time, dissatisfaction with you, or any number of other reasons). Don't focus on this segment, focus instead on the 60%!

That 60% chunk in the middle is a huge pile of referrals waiting to happen, if only you had a plan in place. These customers are happy with you, but won't go out of their way to share that with others, unless you incentivize them to do so. Your company may have some sort of referral in place, but remember: It's easy for customers to ignore companies these days; it's harder for them to ignore a person they like. That means *you* have to do the asking, not your company.

If that 60% block of your customers gave you referrals, would that be worth your time? You bet it would! So what can you do?

Here are some easy ways to generate more referrals.

- Ask! After the sale, I hope you have a follow-up plan already in place. Sometimes a quick call is all it takes, to check in with the buyer. Ask about their satisfaction, thank them, and then ask them for two or three names of people they might be willing to introduce you to, either within the same company, or in other companies. It's important to specify a number "two or three names of people," rather than asking if they can refer you "to anyone." Specifying a number triggers the brain to meet that goal.

- Send a hand-written thank-you card. This stands out in today's printed-label world. Follow up a few days later to make sure it was received, and make the ask for two or three referrals.

- Send a gift. I am always blown away to receive a gift that was thoughtfully selected with me in mind. Two recent ones that stand out: a makeup bag with my initials embroidered on it, and one of those bouquets made entirely from fruit. I guarantee you'll get a response from your client, and that's the perfect time to ask for referrals.

- Be specific. Check out the client's LinkedIn profile to see who they know. If you see some names that would make great customers, ask for an introduction, or at the very least, ask if you can reach out to those people and use your client's name (or better yet, copy the client in an introductory email).

- Motivate your buyers to refer you by holding a contest. It may seem a little cheesy, but there's no denying that it works.

- Motivate your buyers to refer you by giving a Starbucks gift card for every introduction.

What's your plan going forward to generate more referrals from your 60%? Write specific action steps below.

The Coffee Introduction

The third way buyers most like to meet a new salesperson is over coffee. This may be a bit surprising to you, because I'm sure you've tried to get many prospects to join you for coffee or lunch, but you've never been rejected more than in the past three years. Don't worry, it's not you. It's them.

Buyers prefer the calm, casual environment of a coffee appointment because it's not as much of a commitment as lunch. Nevertheless, buyers are rushed, overworked, and hard-pressed to get 30 minutes to leave the office to meet you on the off chance they might do business with you, so you have to be strategic. Here are some tips.

- In your email, keep the subject line vague and brief. I like "Coffee?" or "Coffee later this month?"
- Send a group email to two or three people in the same organization. Usually, they will "appoint" one of them to be the spokesperson to meet with you, so the others don't

have to. Either way, one is better than none.

- If you're being ignored via email, you'll have a huge success rate if you send a hand-written card with a $5 or $10 coffee gift card inside. Why hand-written? Because envelopes from strangers with printed labels on them get thrown away, plain and simple.
- Not in the same city? That's OK. Send a gift card and invite the prospect to have "virtual coffee" with you via Skype!

Connecting on LinkedIn

The fourth-most preferred way you can connect with buyers is via LinkedIn. You may be sensing that buyers are becoming more resistant to LinkedIn as a prospecting tool, and you're right. That's because salespeople abused it for years, and broke the two cardinal rules of LinkedIn prospecting: 1) they sent out heaps of generic connection requests and 2) they went straight for the sale rather than making a human connection first.

Clearly though, buyers are still open to LinkedIn, according to my research, so definitely use it, but use it correctly.

- When you connect with someone new, never send a generic connection request using LinkedIn's pre-populated verbiage. Always personalize your message by mentioning a mutual connection or referring to something from the prospect's profile that caught your eye. Yes, it takes time, but your success rate will go from less than 10% with a generic request, to upwards of 50-75% with a personalized one.
- Don't go for the sale too early. With any of the social media platforms out there, the goal is to be social. Slow it down, and remember the S.P.A.D.E.S. formula.
- If you've been in sales for more than 10 years, you know the benefit of combing through magazines, finding prospects who've been mentioned or recognized, and sending them the page from the magazine along

with a note of congratulations. While this is still an appreciated gesture, you can move your efforts to LinkedIn. If you see a list of award recipients, reach out to those who are potential prospects, inviting them to connect along with a brief message of congratulations.

- If your prospect has less than 500 connections on LinkedIn, just be aware that they probably don't use it very often, and you might need a different route to reach her.

NOTE: Did you know that you can download a spreadsheet of your entire list of LinkedIn connections, along with their email addresses? Google it!

Small Gifts in the Mail

About half of buyers surveyed said they'd welcome a small gift in the mail as a way for salespeople to make initial contact. My #1 tip when it comes to mailing something is this: Nobody throws away lumpy mail. Think about it! If you get something that's in a padded envelope or of a strange shape, you would never throw it away without checking it out first.

My #2 tip is people are far less likely to throw away an envelope with a hand-written address. It's from an actual human being, and triggers something that demands at least opening the envelope.

There are endless ideas for small gifts. I've received microwave popcorn from a company promoting a film festival. I've received red, white and blue confetti for Independence Day. The point is to stand out, and anything thoughtful, unusual and/or lumpy does the trick.

Unsolicited Email

While 43% of surveyed buyers said they prefer an unsolicited email as their first point of introduction to a salesperson, be wary. You know from personal experience how many buyers ignore your emails. My suspicion is buyers say they prefer this method, because it is the easiest for them to weed through and clear out of their path—everything else, like phone calls and coffee appointments, takes time.

My advice about email contains many specific suggestions later in this book. I still believe that email done correctly is a good entry point to a prospect. Email blasts and impersonal, salesy emails are quickly fading, though, so don't spend a lot of time on those.

Cold Calls

Cold calling is preferred by less than 25% of prospects. That means it's a turn-off for three-fourths of your prospects!

As I showed in a previous bar chart, less than 10% of buyers ever pick up the phone anymore, so be careful here. As with email, I believe buyers who indicate they prefer cold calls (much like those who indicated they prefer unsolicited emails) prefer them because they're easy to ignore and weed through on a busy day. It doesn't mean

25% of them still pick up the phone, so don't be fooled.

But…don't throw your phone in the trash yet! You can still call prospects, but you have to be much savvier about your approach these days, and it's got a name: Intelligence Calling. I give specific examples later in the toolkit section.

The Unexpected Pop-In Visit

This is the most-hated method of prospecting by all the buyers surveyed. It's like knocking on someone's door at home to sell something. Do you trust that person? Nope. Does it annoy you? Yep.

For God's sake, just don't do this anymore.

A caveat: If you have a scheduled appointment with someone in their office, and you've been wanting to meet one of their colleagues, ask for a quick introduction. Don't be salesy, don't shove a brochure into their hands, just meet in person, mention something you know about them, or mention a friend you have in common. Then respectfully leave them to the rest of their day. Your follow-up will be much more well received.

What About Social Selling?

When you hear "social selling," you might think of Facebook, LinkedIn, Twitter, and a number of others. You'd be partially right. Those are social media platforms, but they're just a component of social selling.

Social selling is a mindset and a philosophy. It's using the tools at your disposal (both traditional like email, and newer tools like LinkedIn) to build relationships differently.

Wikipedia defines it this way:

"Social selling is the process of developing relationships as part of the sales process. Today this often takes place via social networks such as LinkedIn, Twitter, Facebook, and Pinterest, but can take place either online or offline. Examples of social selling techniques include sharing relevant content, interacting directly with potential buyers and customers, personal branding, and social listening."

I liken it to a cocktail party. You wouldn't walk into a party, canvas the room with business cards, and walk out. You'd quickly be ignored and forgotten.

Rather, you walk in, introduce yourself, build rapport, ask a lot of questions, and show genuine interest in the other people you meet. You find out about their unique challenges and opportunities. You offer advice, connections, and solutions. This stranger begins to trust and like you. When they have a need, they're now more likely to reach out to you. They're also more likely to refer you, because they know you as a human being. *That's* social selling.

Why is it so important today? Simple: "Social sellers realize 66% greater quota attainment than those using traditional selling techniques." (Source:www.salesforlife.com/blog/4-major-objections-every-sales-leader-has-about-social-selling)

Social media platforms like Facebook and Twitter are just newer ways to find, connect with, and learn about prospects, so you can practice social selling.

Breaking Through to the Buyer

It's harder than ever to break through the media overload and get through to your prospects today. The end goal is still the same: You've got to build relationships, but how?

How do you become someone who matters to us? The tools are simple; the mindset is simple. It's just a matter of releasing the old thought patterns and tossing away your old selling playbook.

You're reading this book because you feel this undercurrent. You know something's got to change. You're looking for tools to help you work smarter, not harder, right? Who really wants to work harder?! Who has the capacity these days to work harder than they already are, anyway?

The whole key to prospecting is becoming part of our circle to become someone whose communications don't get ignored or deleted.

So what does that mean to you as a salesperson? It means you have to become part of my *community*, you have to become a *peer* of mine in order for me to trust you.

How do you do that?

Don't be the proverbial guy who patrols the cocktail party like a shark. This isn't about quantity anymore, it's about quality. Be the guy who shows genuine interest, is personable, and not just about the next sale. That's the type of salesperson who attracts today's tough prospects into his circle of trust.

Your buyers will make time for human connections done the right way. By ignoring your traditional sales tactics, your buyers are telling you that the way you're trying to make those connections isn't working for them.

You have to become part of their community—and that is *not* by leading with your company. I'm going to distrust most of you right out of the gate if you come at me as your company. You can't do that anymore.

Your features and benefits don't matter to me until you, as a person, matter to me.

Do you trust ads on TV? Nope. Most of us these days don't trust anyone or anything overtly trying to sell to us. You'll notice a big change in Super Bowl ads from five or 10 years ago, for example—they don't try to sell. The good ones try to evoke emotion, which builds trust and memorability with a brand. In a sense, these ads are *marketing,* not selling!

I bet before you make a major purchase these days, you do a little research online, ask your friends and family, maybe read customer review sites. You don't just go out and buy a Toyota because a Toyota commercial said their car is the best.

By that same token, your buyers don't take your word for it anymore. It's all becoming more social. What do my peers say? What does the community say? What do your current and former buyers say?

This is what social selling is about! It's not just rattling off how great your company is and pushing a PDF brochure into my inbox. It doesn't work that way anymore.

There's a caveat that if I have a specific need at that exact moment in time for what you happen to be selling to me, then your glossy brochure might have a sliver of chance of getting me to respond. Other than that, I am so hyper-focused on what's right in front of me, I don't have time, and your glossy brochure gets tossed in the virtual trash. You haven't made it into my circle of peers, and thus, you and your brochure are easy to ignore.

You can keep selling the traditional way, but I know you're feeling this evolution and I know you're struggling with it. The thing is, a lot of salespeople believe that it's their fault. "Well, if I only call or email more or if I just had better materials or better business cards. It's Marketing's fault. If they just made better brochures, I wouldn't be in this mess."

I'm telling you it's not that. It is not any of that. It is just that your buyers, by and large, have changed. I know many, many bosses and higher-ups at the national and international level are still focusing on traditional sales methods and cracking the whip saying, "You need to log more calls and you need to send out more email blasts…" They're wasting their time and yours.

I hope some of those people will read this, because anyone can make this shift. It's never too late to catch up with where your prospects need you to be.

Section 4

Your New Selling Toolkit

Don't Become Extinct!

12 Tools for Selling Success

In this section, we're going to roll up our sleeves and get to work. Enough about theory and philosophy—let's get specific about the actual tools you can start using today to boost your prospecting and relationship-building effectiveness.

Since we just covered the importance of social selling, let's delve into some of the social media tools that can help you.

1. LinkedIn

LinkedIn is the best tool to happen to prospecting since the dawn of sales. Imagine a place where millions of people list their own résumés, interests, and contacts, all for your viewing pleasure! Most professionals have a profile on LinkedIn these days, so it's a great place to start every time.

As a professional speaker, I'm always seeking to build my circle of contacts. If I hear of a sales conference, I will Google it and see if I can locate a contact name. Then, I always turn to LinkedIn.

LinkedIn used to be fantastic for making an initial connection with a prospect. We were all fascinated in the early days with all these connection requests delivered to our inboxes. Today, it's lost a lot of effectiveness because the sheer volume of connection requests turned off a lot of prospects, and the requests began to get ignored.

Some prospects still respond, but instead of a 95% success rate when LinkedIn was newer, you may get a 50-60% response rate (still really good!).

> *A lot depends on how
> you craft your initial
> connection request.*

Here are a few pointers.

- Never (and I mean *never ever*) send a generic connection request to a prospect. This is the default verbiage that LinkedIn supplies ("I'd like to add you to my professional network on LinkedIn.") when you simply hit "Connect."
- LinkedIn is known for changing its structure frequently, but as of this writing, the only way to customize a connection request is from within someone's profile. Click Connect and the standard field appears, asking how you know the person (Friend, Colleague, etc.). If you connect from a list of people, the invitation is simply sent with no option to write a message. So always visit the person's profile and connect from there.

- When connecting, be sure to review the person's profile, and pick out something to remark upon. This is really important at building rapport, so don't skip it. I like to comment on where they went to college (especially if their college was a rival of mine!), or some mutual friend(s) we have.
- *Don't sell* during this initial connection request. Keep it brief, build rapport, and don't be tempted to mention how great your company or your widget is. Remember the cocktail party analogy—this is just a casual hello. Feel free to drop a compliment, or mention that you wanted to connect because you keep hearing their name, etc.

What do you do when someone accepts your connection request on LinkedIn? I'll tell you what most salespeople do when I accept their connections: Nothing! I never hear from them again.

When a prospect accepts your connection request, I call this "picking up the virtual phone." They have accepted your initial hello, and by doing so, have essentially said "hello" back (although most will rarely type out a message to that effect). Don't leave them hanging!

Within 24 hours (lest they forget who you are), send a quick note thanking them for the connection, and mentioning something else about them that you found interesting in their profile. Build that rapport further.

BEWARE: Most salespeople will use this opportunity to sell, sell, sell. It's still too soon. You're still at that virtual cocktail party, just building rapport!

Social selling is about the conversation, and about selflessly supplying information helpful to your prospects as you build new relationships. If you jump to your features and benefits too quickly, you've just categorized yourself with the other guys who are too eager. You've lost a great opportunity to humanize yourself and become part of that prospect's community.

Let me give you three fictitious examples.

Example 1

A salesperson from a software company sends a generic invitation to connect with me. I perhaps glance at her profile, but seeing no connection with her, and having nothing else to help me decide, it's just easier to delete the request—she's just trying to sell me something. When I need software, I'll seek it out.

Example 2

A salesperson from a software company sends me a nice invitation to connect, mentioning a mutual acquaintance. I accept. I receive back a lengthy message all about his fabulous software and its features and benefits. Too soon! He should have spent a little time researching my company, and responded back by sharing a few tidbits to demonstrate he's done his homework. He should still be in the rapport- and trust-building phase, but he skipped over that part and went straight for the sale. How does he know his features and benefits will address any of my current challenges, when he doesn't know what my current challenges are?

Example 3

A salesperson from a software company sends me a nice invitation to connect, mentioning a mutual acquaintance. I accept. I never hear from that salesperson again. When I do have a need, I've forgotten the name of the salesperson and the name of the software, so I start my search from scratch on Google. Opportunity lost.

Keep in mind when you're reaching out on LinkedIn to slow down and cultivate the relationship; don't go for the quick sale because it rarely happens that way.

Homework: send authentic, non-salesy connection requests to 50 prospects. Track how many have responded within one week. If it's fewer than 50%, rethink what you write in your invitation.

Your LinkedIn Profile

I can't discuss LinkedIn without a brief visit to your profile. It's shocking to me how many salespeople have a profile set up entirely to land their next job, not their next client.

When you're crafting your LinkedIn summary section, write it with your prospects in mind. Don't talk about how great you are at hitting your quotas, how many sales awards you've won, or how you love to close. These are all turn-offs to your prospects!

Instead, answer these questions to humanize yourself and demonstrate that you can be a trusted peer:

- What was the first job you ever had in your current industry (or your first job ever)? How did you evolve into your current role? Sometimes it's great to share that first awful job you had, since we've all had them! It makes you highly relatable if you were a busboy who eventually evolved to be a salesperson in the restaurant industry.

- What are you most passionate about, with regard to your job? What gets you up in the morning? What do you love most about working with clients?
- What's a lesson you learned the hard way? Talking about a failure is very humanizing.
- Share something personal, i.e. "When I'm not at work, I love to fish with my son, go to Iowa Hawkeye sports events, and spend time with my incredible wife of 22 years.

Homework: Your LinkedIn profile is critical, so get it in the best shape possible!

Do You Need an Upgraded LinkedIn Account?

I do not have an upgraded account myself, and I find I'm able to do everything I want on LinkedIn. I know salespeople who swear by their premium accounts because they have access to unlocked features and more robust searches. You can accomplish a lot with a free account, though. My recommendation is to keep it free until it no longer accomplishes your goals, and then try the 30-day free upgrade to see if it truly makes a difference for you.

2. The Trifecta

tri·fect·a
trī'fektə/

"A perfect group of three; winning three times." [Source: www.urbandictionary.com]

Today, cold calling by itself just doesn't cut it. You know that. There is a process you can use that will increase the effectiveness of your calling time, and I call it The Trifecta. This is originally a betting term (well, horse racing, to be exact), but I borrow it here to show you that you can increase those prospecting odds by following my process.

As you might have guessed, The Trifecta has three steps:

1) Step one is to visit the prospect's LinkedIn profile. Peruse the profile to pick out something you have in common, or something interesting you noticed, like where they went to school, a mutual connection you share, etc. Connect with the prospect using the specific LinkedIn techniques I outline in Section 4.

2) Step Two is to call the prospect. You will likely go to their voicemail. In your message, it's important to mention that a) you just sent them a LinkedIn invitation, and b) you will follow up with

an email. Don't be salesy.

3) Step Three is to email the prospect. I prefer the subject line, "Per My Voicemail." People tend to open these. In your email, mention the LinkedIn invitation and the voicemail. I prefer to make a joke about the flood of communications I'm sending them, and then keep it casual by telling them I simply wasn't sure what their preferred communication method was. (hint: however they respond back...that's their preferred method of communication!).

Voila – The Trifecta! You'll certainly get noticed by the prospect, who hopefully will respect the amount of effort you've invested into starting a relationship.

I know what you're thinking...'this Trifecta business is going to take triple the time.' I know it's more time consuming, but it's way more productive time.

If you make 25 traditional cold calls in an hour, with the established 96% failure rate, that means one person answers the phone, and the rest never call you back. Using The Trifecta, you might complete only 10 of the three-step processes, but I bet you hear back from half of them. That means you'll connect with five people in that same hour, versus one using traditional cold calling. A 500% increase in your productivity in the same amount of time!

3. Facebook

While LinkedIn currently is the best social media site for quality business prospecting, Facebook is the largest. Think of it as quality versus quantity.

Should you be using Facebook for business? The answer, in my opinion, is yes, unless your target demographic is under 25. This age group is largely moving away from Facebook in favor of Snapchat, Instagram, and others.

I'm not suggesting you actively market on Facebook; I'm suggesting you use it as one of your many tools to humanize yourself to prospects.

I've been asked by many salespeople if they should accept friend requests from prospects and clients, and my answer is always a resounding "yes!" That's the best sign you're moving into the trusted peer category, and as I've been saying, that's the best possible place for a salesperson to be these days.

You'll recall I spoke earlier about the blurring of lines between our business and personal lives, and Facebook is the biggest culprit. It can be a fantastic tool to build relationships with prospects, and strengthen ties with current clients, if used correctly. That means being careful about what you share, so you're never offensive or overly personal with people you don't know well.

Facebook allows you to separate your Friends into groups, so you can easily segregate your close friends away from your prospects and customers, and share posts more selectively.

Homework: If you've already blurred the lines between friends and customers, now might be a great time to segment them into different groups. Then when you accept new Friend requests, you can easily place them into the appropriate category going forward.

A Cautionary Facebook Tale...

I have a friend who is a fellow speaker, and she is constantly posting on Facebook about work, and nothing but work. I never get to see her post anything "real" about her family, her weekend, her holidays. She seems very unapproachable as a result, which is not the case at all in person. So if you must separate your social audiences, be careful that you still show a little humanity.

4. Twitter

Is Twitter worth your time as a salesperson? The answer is: it depends. What's your demographic?

While I'm active on Twitter, I don't spend much time on it. I've automated most of my posts using a free tool called www.TwitterFeed.com. It allows me to connect my account to a number of different media outlets, and when a new blog or article is posted by the media outlet, a tweet is automatically generated from me to my followers.

I only tweet live when I'm attending a conference, or speaking at one. I've found this combination of automated and live postings to be the best use of my time. The automated posts help me position myself as an expert-in-the-know, and the live posts remind people that I'm human.

I don't believe Twitter is actively generating a lot of new relationships for salespeople, for several reasons:

- If your target demographic is primarily business professionals, they aren't on Twitter during the business day.

- The way Twitter works, your tweets don't wait in someone's inbox to be read or seen. Your window for tweets to be seen is very slim, as a result.
- Because of abuse by spammers, Direct Messages sent on Twitter are largely ignored these days, because users don't expect them to be legitimate.
- Of the 1.3 billion Twitter accounts, only 320 million are active (source: www.brandwatch.com). That means that you may not have the followers you think you have.

All in all, I believe Twitter is a fading social media tool, and there's likely a better use of your time where social selling is concerned. Still, if you prefer to use Twitter, there are some things that can help you connect better with prospects:

- Don't send Direct Messages. If you want to reach someone, just tweet them openly.

- If you're targeting a prospect on Twitter, check when they sent their last tweet. If it's been more than a month, you're wasting your time.
- Retweet your prospects. Comment, tweet case studies or business intelligence relevant to something they've just tweeted. Start conversations based on something you've learned about a prospect.
- Twitter is a good tool for Social Listening. This means gathering intelligence on prospects so that you can form stronger relationships however you ultimately connect (LinkedIn, Twitter, email, phone, etc.).
- "Research has shown that Tweets with photos get 313% more engagement." (Source: blog.twitter.com/2015/tweettip-use-photos-to-drive-engagement)

5. YouTube

YouTube is second only to Facebook in the number of active users per month (Source: www.smartinsights.com/social-media-marketing/social-media-strategy/new-global-social-media-research/).

This is a great tool to reach your prospects and clients in the most humanizing way possible, if done correctly. Now that you know the critical importance of gathering Social Proof in the form of video testimonials from happy clients, you've got one solid use for YouTube. The second use is to proactively add content to your channel that will appeal to your buyers.

What kind of content is appealing? That depends on what keeps your customers awake at night. What frustrates them in their job? What solutions can you offer in a non-salesy way to make their lives better?

Record yourself sharing ideas, resources and solutions in short videos. Interview experts or customers. Show cool new features or uses of your product.

Keep in mind people like to consume videos that are brief, so you don't need to wax poetic for an hour at a time!

According to a Wistia.com report (https://wistia.com/blog/optimal-video-length), keeping your videos under two minutes in length is ideal as far as the highest level of engagement is concerned. After that, the second most preferred length is anywhere from 6-12 minutes.

Also, keep your content evergreen, meaning try not to mention dates or trends that may make your video outdated before its time.

Lastly, keep your content fresh. Add something new at least every month or two, if not more frequently.

6 & 7. Instagram & Pinterest

I've grouped these two social media together, because they have similar traits – they're both very visual. These tools are worth your time if what you're selling is:

a) A visual product or service
b) Targeted at Millennials or women

Like Facebook, the goal here isn't to push your company, it's to build rapport, but these tools also allow you to build awareness of what you're selling. Be cautious not to be overtly salesy, as users will be turned off rather quickly.

8. Snapchat

This is the newest tool that I'll be addressing. While it's been largest embraced by younger generations, its business uses are just beginning to be tapped. If you are targeting a younger demographic and have some extra time to dabble with Snapchat, follow the guidelines I've set forth with other tools: humanize yourself, don't be too salesy, and share relevant content.

9. Email that Gets Opened

I've done extensive research on what gets buyers to respond to email these days, and I've learned some tips that you can use.

Email subject lines are critical. More people check email on mobile devices today than on computers, meaning you have only the space of a subject line to grab attention and avoid deletion.

NOTE: I've prepared a free bonus whitepaper on the 100 best and worst email subject lines I've received. Download it at

www.shawnasuck ow.com/100

I have found with email subject lines, intrigue works best. I recommend short, vague questions. These beg to be opened out of sheer curiosity, and then you've got the buyer's attention for a split second.

You've made it past the moat, now you have to cross the drawbridge! Keeping the buyer's attention is tough. Instead of salesy, overly-hyped verbiage, just talk like a real person. Keep it brief, tell them how you know them, share something you've discovered about them personally or professionally, and ask for further action.

Many sales emails tell me they will follow up in a couple days. That's too soon! Give me at least a week if you're going to follow up with me. If you're asking for a call or a coffee meeting, give me at least two weeks. Buyers' calendars, like yours, are fuller than ever.

In your email, ask HOW and WHEN you should follow up, and then respect what the buyer says. If I tell a salesperson to follow up in three months, I don't want to hear from them in 30 days. The exception is a casual email with a bit of helpful information UNRELATED to your product or service – something you thought I might find helpful or interesting from my industry, for example.

An Email Case Study

Let me tell you the story of David, a salesperson for a technology company. David cold-called me one day, telling me about his fabulous software. Then he reached out again. And again. And again. Then the emails started coming. David was relentless, and I never responded.

Then, one day, David sent a different kind of email. He said he was sitting in the waiting room at the hospital, awaiting the birth of his first grandchild. He had plenty of time on his hands, because his daughter's labor was long. He was trying to keep his mind occupied, so he thought he'd follow up with me.

That email stopped me in my tracks! I took notice. I read it, and I responded. Why? Because that day,

David was no longer a SALESperson, he was a person. A person I could relate to.

Email Blasts

Email blasts are the worst way for a salesperson to connect with prospects. Leave these to the marketing department. If you ARE the marketing department too, here are some tips to help you out:

- Remove the typical mention at the top of an email blast that gives away the fact that it's a mass email. These include links to unsubscribe, or to open the email in a browser. You can always put these mentions at the bottom of your email blast.
- Remove any formatting, colors, borders, or columns, so that the email blast looks just like a regular, person-to-person email.
- Attempt to personalize the email as much as possible, even though it's a blast. If you can personalize more than the recipient's first name, do so. This means extra work, but it will be worth the extra time so your

recipients think they're receiving a personal email from you. You can do this by customizing a merge field with something like how you met, where you last saw them, etc.

- Your subject line is critical, so use the previous tips in your email blasts as well.

Video Email

We pay attention to things that are different, correct? That's why you should give video email a try. This is simply using your smart phone to video yourself saying whatever you normally would write in an email, and forwarding it to your client or prospect via email. Yes, it's still arriving to them via email, but it looks different so it's likely to get opened. You simply send a bit of a written explanation in the body of the email so the recipient isn't confused or doesn't think it's spam.

There are services like www.BombBomb.com that make video email really user-friendly. You can communicate with clients back and forth via BombBomb, using their video tool on your laptop or phone, and everything is stored for your records. You also get notified when the recipient has watched your message. There is a free version with ads and limitations, or you can upgrade for a small annual fee to eliminate ads and have more flexibility, like sending a video email blast to up to 3,000 users at once, and attaching documents as well.

Your Email Signature Block

Your email signature block is prime real estate. Are you using it to its maximum effectiveness? Consider including:

- Your photo. This is the most humanizing thing you can include. Make sure the photo captures your friendliest, most approachable self possible. Avoid what I call the "5th grade posed photo" with the cloudy gray or blue background. Smile with your eyes!
- A link to all the Social Proof you'll be gathering with your phone!

I've described the importance of gathering video testimonials, and this is just one place to share your collection. Put a link to your website or your YouTube channel, and make sure your testimonials are always fresh and not outdated.

- A link to a recent whitepaper.
- A link to you in the news. Have you received an award or been quoted in a publication?

Homework: rewrite your email signature block to be as attractive as possible to buyers.

10. Video Calls

I've talked about video email and its emerging usefulness, so now let's talk about video calls using tools like Skype, Facetime, and www.zoom.us (my personal preference).

(Note: for brevity, I'll use Skype as an umbrella term for video calls in this section, although there are many great alternatives, both existing and emerging).

If a picture speaks a thousand words, a video surely speaks millions. Live video is the next best thing to being in person with someone, so it's shocking to me how few salespeople use Skype as a business tool.

We're all familiar with Skype as a way to chat with Grandma, but it has serious business value. I've talked about the importance of humanizing yourself, and nothing is better than seeing someone in the flesh.

I heard a great strategy from a salesperson who connects with his prospects when he is in the midst of writing a proposal for them. He asks them to Skype with him so he can go over a few things. As he's on the video call, he's establishing rapport, and asking them for their advice on the way to craft his proposal to win the bid. He's amazingly successful at getting his prospects to give him important insights into the hot button issues of decision-makers, because he takes the time to ask the right questions. There's no doubt that the face-to-face comfort level established through Skype is part of his success.

Skype Success Tips

- Check out your background, and make sure you're sending the right message to your Skype viewers. Your office should have a good mix of professionalism and a few personal touches. These are conversation-starters and rapport-builders!
- Don't Skype someone without an appointment to do so. It's an intrusion.
- When you ask someone to Skype with you, they might be caught off-guard, because they likely don't see Skype as a business tool, either. Some prospects are nervous about using this type of technology as well. I recommend saying something like, "Hey, should we try Skyping sometime? I've been wanting to try it on my new computer."
- If you want a fun tactic to get someone to say yes to a Skype appointment, drop a Starbucks

$5 gift card in the mail (make sure it's a hand-written envelope), and inside, ask the recipient to join you for 'virtual coffee.'

- If you are attending a great conference, or unveiling a new product, why not bring your customer along via Skype for a little preview?

Homework: get your office in shape for viewers, and then schedule three Skype calls with existing customers. Once you're comfortable, schedule five Skype calls with prospects.

11. Intelligence Calls

While I clearly don't recommend cold calling, if you must pick up the phone to reach out to someone you've never met, and you don't have time for The Trifecta, what I can recommend is an Intelligence Call. These are well-researched calls. Don't just work a list.

Smiling-and-dialing is so last century!

One of the number one pet peeves of buyers everywhere is that they're annoyed when salespeople have done no prior research before reaching out to them. Go on LinkedIn, or Google the buyer, and be ready to demonstrate that you've come prepared. Then, when you leave the inevitable voice mail, you can let the buyer know you're not like most salespeople.

I also recommend when you leave a voice mail, you reference the one or two other ways you plan to reach out. Tell them you've sent a LinkedIn connection request, and that you're sending them an email as well. When you do, don't make those about your company. Use those rare opportunities to build rapport:

- Mention a common connection you have on LinkedIn
- Share something you've learned about the buyer

- Don't be uber-professional and send an email with a bunch of features and benefits.
- Humanize yourself in the eyes of the buyer. It's easy to ignore a company; it's harder to ignore a human being.

12. Getting Results at Events

Trade Shows

Trade shows are a great way to generate new leads, but there are shifts in consumer preferences in this arena as well. This may seem exactly the opposite of what you usually do, but don't spend valuable time with a buyer talking about your product or service. Spend that time gathering as much information as you can, so your follow-up is more than "Here's my brochure, it was nice to meet you."

In the era of the buyer, the salesperson with the most information on the buyer's challenges, frustrations and successes wins. Typically, salespeople see a prospect in their booth and think they have to throw as much information at the buyer as possible, given that this may be their only chance. Wrong! Get to know the buyer. Ask questions. Show interest. Ask what keeps them up at night. Then use that intelligence in your follow-up with the most targeted information possible. The buyer feels heard, and your solution is evident.

If you have arranged for a prospect to visit your booth for an appointment, try this: Google the buyer in advance, check out her LinkedIn profile, and create a dossier on her. Don't start the conversation with "here's my product." Start with "here's what I've learned about you." Buyers will be impressed.

Customer Appreciation Events

In my opinion, live events are the best tool to generate awareness, build relationships, and breed loyalty. If your company will allow you the ability to hold a customer appreciation event, by all means, do it. Even if it's just a simple holiday luncheon for your 10 best customers, it's of great value. Your customers will feel valued, and they'll have the opportunity to connect with other customers of yours for networking opportunities.

Customer Advisory Board

This is a great type of event to achieve two goals: 1) make your customers feel important and appreciated, and 2) get insight into their current challenges and opportunities.

If you don't stay on top of your marketplace and your customers' needs, you're leaving yourself vulnerable to other salespeople who will. Consider holding an annual or biannual event to check in with your best customers.

Other Tools with Big Results

Your Voicemail Greeting

Most salespeople don't give their voicemail greeting a second thought. They record it once when they get the job, and then forget about it unless they change it to go on vacation.

If your voicemail greeting sounds anything like this: 'Hi, you've reached my voicemail. Sorry I missed your call. Please leave your name, number, and a brief message, and I'll return your call as soon as possible," then you're missing a big opportunity to differentiate yourself!

If you represent a hotel, for example, why not try this: "Hi, I'd love to take your call, but I'm out showing a client our beautiful new ballroom."

If you sell cars: "Hi, I'm out test-driving the new Tesla model – I'm happy to give you a full report when I return your call."

If you sell banking services: "Hi, I'm probably helping one of our 2,000 small business customers to set up a new HSA or SEP account. I'll tell you about our new rates when I return your call.

If you're going on vacation, use this as an opportunity to build rapport! "Hi, I'm out until the 7th, barreling down the slopes in Vail, trying to avoid a visit to the E.R." When you return from vacation, don't you think your customers will remember this, and probably ask you about it?

Homework: change that stale voicemail greeting!

Your Email Auto-Reply

This is another overlooked sales tool! When you go on vacation, you probably add an automatic notification to your email, letting people know you're out. Why not use this as an opportunity to build rapport?

Case Study: The Grandma

This is one of the best auto-replies I've ever received:

"Your email is important to me. I'm currently in sunny California with grandsons ages 5 and 6. If it's urgent and you don't mind children playing and dogs in the background, call my cell at XXX-XXX-XXXX. Otherwise, I will respond to your email when I return on Tuesday afternoon a much more relaxed person."

This is fantastic for several reasons!

- Anyone with grandchildren or a grandmother will immediately relate to her.

- This humanizes her in a fantastic, relatable way. Don't you like her immediately??
- If you need something from her and she's not available, aren't you more likely to cut her some slack? If she were a nameless, faceless person, you might get irritated that she's not available, but not Grandma!
- When she returns your email, what's the first question you're going to ask her? "How was your visit with your grandsons?" You betcha.

This woman accomplished so much by just being authentic where most people would think, "Oh I can't share that, it's too personal." In this era of S.P.A.D.E.S., she has shown authenticity and differentiated herself beautifully, cheaply, and easily. Brilliant.

Homework: Next time you need to use an email auto-reply, come up with something creative!

The Last Word

It's easy to ignore a company, but harder to ignore a living, breathing human being with whom we can relate. What this crazy era is telling you as a salesperson is this: be human, be relatable, and don't be overtly salesy.

Your role is to champion your customer, not your company anymore. This is a huge shift in mindset, but if you truly believe this, it shows, and your customers will be attracted to that.

Keep in mind buyers today are waiting until the last minute to contact sales, or even trying to bypass you altogether. That doesn't leave you much room to influence the typical buyer, so you can no longer be the typical salesperson. Extinction is approaching for them...

If you're the one buyers trust, they'll keep you in their inner circle. This means no extinction for you. This means constant referrals because you're striving to remain relevant. You're doing your research, keeping abreast of what keeps your customers awake at night, and you're out to solve their problems.

You're not going to become extinct because you realize that selling has a new mindset today: listen 90% of the time, and use the other 10% to provide solutions, not features or benefits.

Yes, you are going to be among the minority who not only survive, but thrive in the new era of customer-centric sales. Why? Because you're not just going to put this book down and forget what you've just learned. You're going to thrive, because you're among the few who are going to write down changes you're willing to make, and commit to taking action.

Three changes I'm going to make today:

1. _____

2. _____

3. _____

Three changes I'm going to make in the next week:

1. _____

2. _____

3. _____

Three changes I'm going to make in the next month:

1. _____

2. _____

3. _____

Three changes I'm going to make in the upcoming year:

1. _____

2. _____

3. _____

Congratulations!

Now go forth and thrive, because you're no dinosaur.

Love the book?
Unlock the full program!

I know, after finishing this book, your head is probably full of To Do's and Oh No's. You're already a sales rock star, but you want to up your game. Where to start? What to do?

I'm here to help! I've created a six-week Master Class to guide you through all the branding and prospecting shifts you'll want to make to master the new era of sales and blow the lid off your past performance. This Master Class includes:

> **6 weeks of streamed content - work at your own pace**
> **A full week dedicated to each of the S.P.A.D.E.S. principles**
> **Simple, focused tasks to keep you on target**
> **Tips & tricks to skyrocket your sales results!**

PLUS TWO BONUSES FOR MY READERS
(available for a limited time!):

> **A private Facebook community for support**
> **Weekly Q&A opportunities with Shawna**

shawnasuckow.com/MasterClass

BUYER SECRETS REVEALED!

SPEAKER • AUTHOR • BUYER INSIDER©

Shawna has wowed audiences of sales professionals and business leaders on five continents. She tells it like it is, with humor and matter-of-factness, pulling back the curtain on how today's buyers really think.

You've heard countless sales speakers who've never been on the professional buyer side. Now it's time to hear the one speaker who brings 20 years of million-dollar buyer experience to your audience.

651.470.0066
www.shawnasuckow.com

About the Author

Shawna Suckow was a million-dollar buyer for more than 20 years. She's the founder of SPIN (Senior Planners Industry Network), a professional association with more than 3,000 members who control nearly $5 billion in purchasing power.

Today, she speaks to business audiences all over the world to help them understand buyer evolution, how to reach prospects in a media-saturated era, and how to sell more to American buyers in particular. To book Shawna for your event, email **info@shawnasuckow.com**.

Shawna's honors include being named to the global list of Top 100 Women Business & Tech Speakers (alongside Hilary Clinton and Lisa Ling!), and Planners' Favorite Speakers list (with James Earl Jones!). This is her third book.

When she's not speaking to sales groups, you can find her at home in Minnesota with her husband, Greg (who incidentally is

Iowa's famous Hawkeye Elvis – Google it!), their two teenagers (who are experts at actively ignoring her and each other), and their dogs Henry (a Golden Retriever who is a trouble-maker) & Gabby (a Black Lab who is a Canadian hockey fan).

Other Books by Shawna, available on Amazon:
- *Planner Pet Peeves (a #1 Best Seller!)*
- *Supplier Pet Peeves (a #2 Best Seller. Not as good as #1, but I'll take it!)*

Bulk discounts on all my books are available starting at just 25 copies.

Connect with Shawna!

Website: **www.thebuyerinsider.com**
Email: **info@shawnasuckow.com**
Twitter: **@shawnasuckow**
Facebook: **Shawna Suckow International**

Made in the USA
Columbia, SC
18 March 2019